C1

THINK-A-GRAMS

EVELYNE M. GRAHAM

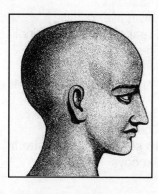

© 1986
THE CRITICAL THINKING CO.
(BRIGHT MINDS™)
www.CriticalThinking.com
P.O. Box 1610 • Seaside • CA 93955-1610
Phone 800-458-4849 • FAX 831-393-3277
ISBN 0-89455-331-3
Reproduction rights granted for single-classroom use only.
Printed in the United States of America

TEACHER SUGGESTIONS AND ANSWERS

SUGGESTIONS

THINK-A-GRAMS are verbal picture puzzles. They can be posted individually, either daily or weekly, on a bulletin board to sharpen students' thinking.

In terms of difficulty, the A level is easiest, B more difficult, and the C level is hardest. Within levels, books 1 and 2 are of similar difficulty.

Each of the books in this series contains an answer key and 100 page-size puzzles. The puzzles provide teachers with an entertaining and challenging tool for coordinating right-brain thinking with left-brain memory. To solve these puzzles, the right brain analyzes the puzzle's symbology and the left brain recalls the common term or phrase depicted.

Since schools devote so much curricula to such left-brain activities as memorization and regurgitation, exposure to more right-brain experiences, such as these THINK-A-GRAMS, helps students develop skills in spatial relations, creative thinking, and problem solving.

Keep in mind that there is frequently more than one answer to a given problem. Encourage students to invent their own THINK-A-GRAMS for your classroom!

ABOUT THE AUTHOR

EVELYNE GRAHAM has 34 years of teaching experience—including all 12 grades—with a major discipline in mathematics. She spent 20 years as Supervisor of Mathematics for Chesapeake Public School System (Virginia), 6 years as Assistant Principal of Instruction at Chesapeake Alternative School, and 10 years as an extension instructor in Mathematics for Elementary Teachers for the University of Virginia.

Mrs. Graham holds an undergraduate degree with triple majors in math, religious education, and music, a masters degree in Mathematics Education, and a Certificate of Advanced Study in School Administration.

Mrs. Graham is a frequent presenter at state and national conferences and the author of books and articles about mathematics education and activities.

ANSWERS C1

1. Task at hand
2. Nerves on edge
3. Top of Old Smoky
4. Broad daylight
5. Break the fall
6. Teaching by example
7. Held in high esteem
8. Written request in triplicate
9. A ton of bricks
10. Coincide
11. Going by the book
12. To be between jobs
13. Weeding the garden
14. Proposal on bended knee
15. Clever afterthought
16. High priority on education
17. Quarter horse
18. Partly cloudy overhead
19. Let bygones be bygones
20. The difference between nineteen and ten
21. Foresees
22. Biweekly
23. Upheaval
24. The aftermath
25. All by myself
26. A little light on the subject
27. Connecting verbs
28. Hypotenuse
29. A ninety-pound weakling
30. Discussed at length
31. Going in all directions
32. Due in part
33. Top of the morning
34. He's over the hill
35. Bicarbonate
36. Half-nelson
37. A bird in the hand is worth two in the bush
38. All about Eve
39. To be after the fact
40. Life begins at forty
41. Tomorrow afternoon
42. To be in arrears
43. Floating down the river
44. Up and at it
45. An initial start
46. Free at last
47. One-sided opinion
48. Pie in the sky
49. To get at the truth
50. A car in every garage
51. March forth
52. Your heart isn't in it
53. Adage
54. Hang on every word
55. Story behind the scenes
56. Tucson
57. Arch of triumph
58. Debug
59. Five-part miniseries
60. English as a second language
61. Half-wit
62. Coming at you from all directions
63. A hill of beans
64. Triple bypass
65. Looking back over the years
66. Overdrawn account
67. Two ships passing in the night
68. Putting ideas down on paper
69. New invention
70. Ignorant about the issues
71. Lone Ranger
72. A tax increase
73. Held up by a burglar
74. Graduation after twelfth grade
75. Topology
76. Once in a blue moon
77. Initial shock
78. Leave at once
79. Betting on the odds
80. To look after oneself
81. Little by little
82. Background
83. A car covered by a warranty
84. Spoken from the bottom of my heart
85. Once upon a time
86. A backward country
87. A little-known intellectual
88. Midshipman
89. Saved in the nick of time
90. A day at a time
91. Tribal dance
92. Upset over nothing
93. Great day in the morning!
94. Friends in high places
95. Almost well
96. Expenses covered by insurance
97. Executive
98. Bass tuba
99. Double or nothing
100. To separate the men from the boys

FOOT
SHOULDER
HAND TASK
HEAD

©1986 MIDWEST PUBLICATIONS
PACIFIC GROVE, CA. 93950-0448

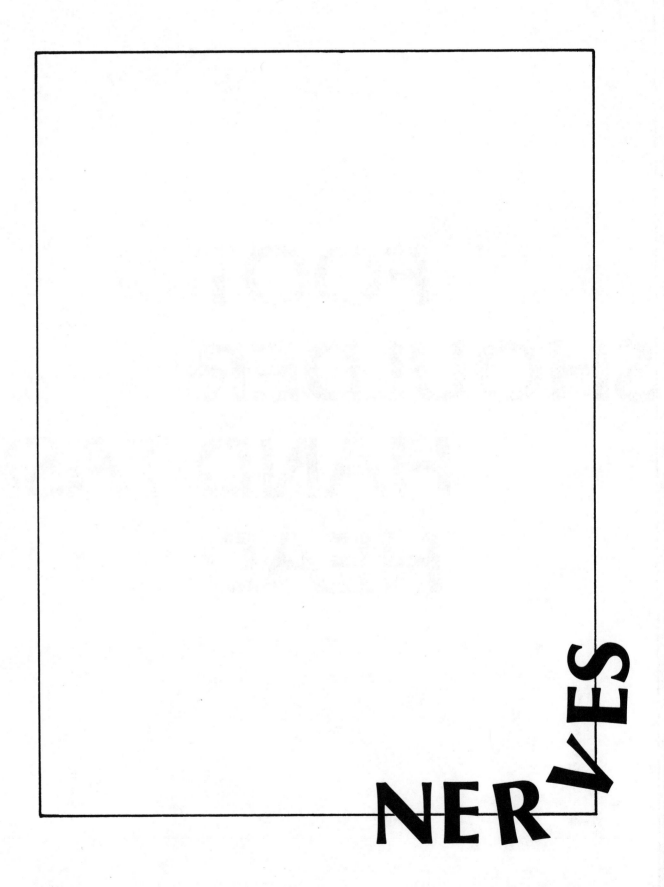

©1986 MIDWEST PUBLICATIONS
PACIFIC GROVE, CA. 93950-0448

©1986 MIDWEST PUBLICATIONS
PACIFIC GROVE, CA. 93950-0448

DAYLIGHT

©1986 MIDWEST PUBLICATIONS
PACIFIC GROVE, CA. 93950-0448

©1986 MIDWEST PUBLICATIONS
PACIFIC GROVE, CA. 93950-0448

TEACHING EXAMPLE

©1986 MIDWEST PUBLICATIONS
PACIFIC GROVE, CA. 93950-0448

ESTHELDEEM

©1986 MIDWEST PUBLICATIONS
PACIFIC GROVE, CA. 93950-0448

TRIPL *request* **ICATE**

©1986 MIDWEST PUBLICATIONS
PACIFIC GROVE, CA. 93950-0448

250 lb.

250 lb.

250 lb.

250 lb.

250 lb.

250 lb.

250 lb.

250 lb.

©1986 MIDWEST PUBLICATIONS
PACIFIC GROVE, CA. 93950-0448

SICODE

©1986 MIDWEST PUBLICATIONS
PACIFIC GROVE, CA. 93950-0448

GOING BOOK

©1986 MIDWEST PUBLICATIONS
PACIFIC GROVE, CA. 93950-0448

JOB BB JOB

©1986 MIDWEST PUBLICATIONS
PACIFIC GROVE, CA. 93950-0448

DING **THE GARDEN**

©1986 MIDWEST PUBLICATIONS
PACIFIC GROVE, CA. 93950-0448

PROPOSAL
KNEE

THOUGHT CLEVER

©1986 MIDWEST PUBLICATIONS
PACIFIC GROVE, CA. 93950-0448

PRIORITY
EDUCATION

©1986 MIDWEST PUBLICATIONS
PACIFIC GROVE, CA. 93950-0448

HORSE
$$\overline{\text{HORSE}}$$
4

©1986 MIDWEST PUBLICATIONS
PACIFIC GROVE, CA. 93950-0448

CLOUDY

HEAD

©1986 MIDWEST PUBLICATIONS
PACIFIC GROVE, CA. 93950-0448

LET GONES
B GONES

©1986 MIDWEST PUBLICATIONS
PACIFIC GROVE, CA. 93950-0448

19 DIFFERENCE 10

©1986 MIDWEST PUBLICATIONS
PACIFIC GROVE, CA. 93950-0448

C C C C

©1986 MIDWEST PUBLICATIONS
PACIFIC GROVE, CA. 93950-0448

KLY
KLY

©1986 MIDWEST PUBLICATIONS
PACIFIC GROVE, CA. 93950-0448

L
A
V
A
E
H

THINK-A-GRAM C1

©1986 MIDWEST PUBLICATIONS
PACIFIC GROVE, CA. 93950-0448

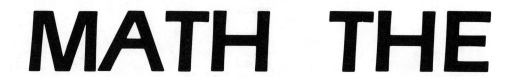

MATH THE

©1986 MIDWEST PUBLICATIONS
PACIFIC GROVE, CA. 93950-0448

ALL MYSELF

©1986 MIDWEST PUBLICATIONS
PACIFIC GROVE, CA. 93950-0448

LIGHT

SUBJECT

©1986 MIDWEST PUBLICATIONS
PACIFIC GROVE, CA. 93950-0448

©1986 MIDWEST PUBLICATIONS
PACIFIC GROVE, CA. 93950-0448

UPOTSE

©1986 MIDWEST PUBLICATIONS
PACIFIC GROVE, CA. 93950-0448

90 lb. KLING

©1986 MIDWEST PUBLICATIONS
PACIFIC GROVE, CA. 93950-0448

WIDTH

HEIGHT

LENGTH DISCUSSED

©1986 MIDWEST PUBLICATIONS
PACIFIC GROVE, CA. 93950-0448

©1986 MIDWEST PUBLICATIONS
PACIFIC GROVE, CA. 93950-0448

©1986 MIDWEST PUBLICATIONS
PACIFIC GROVE, CA. 93950-0448

MORNING

©1986 MIDWEST PUBLICATIONS
PACIFIC GROVE, CA. 93950-0448

©1986 MIDWEST PUBLICATIONS
PACIFIC GROVE, CA. 93950-0448

CARBONATE
CARBONATE

©1986 MIDWEST PUBLICATIONS
PACIFIC GROVE, CA. 93950-0448

NELSON

2

©1986 MIDWEST PUBLICATIONS
PACIFIC GROVE, CA. 93950-0448

HABIRDND
=
BU2SH

©1986 MIDWEST PUBLICATIONS
PACIFIC GROVE, CA. 93950-0448

ALL ALL ALL
ALL ALL
ALL **EVE** ALL
ALL ALL
ALL ALL ALL

©1986 MIDWEST PUBLICATIONS
PACIFIC GROVE, CA. 93950-0448

FACT BB

©1986 MIDWEST PUBLICATIONS
PACIFIC GROVE, CA. 93950-0448

0
10
20
30
40   L
50   I
60   F
        E

©1986 MIDWEST PUBLICATIONS
PACIFIC GROVE, CA. 93950-0448

NOON   TOMORROW

©1986 MIDWEST PUBLICATIONS
PACIFIC GROVE, CA. 93950-0448

©1986 MIDWEST PUBLICATIONS
PACIFIC GROVE, CA. 93950-0448

F
L
O
A   RIVER
T
I
N
G

©1986 MIDWEST PUBLICATIONS
PACIFIC GROVE, CA. 93950-0448

HE
IT   UP AND
SHE

©1986 MIDWEST PUBLICATIONS
PACIFIC GROVE, CA. 93950-0448

S.T.A.R.T.

©1986 MIDWEST PUBLICATIONS
PACIFIC GROVE, CA. 93950-0448

FIRST
SECOND
THIRD
LAST FREE

©1986 MIDWEST PUBLICATIONS
PACIFIC GROVE, CA. 93950-0448

OPINION

©1986 MIDWEST PUBLICATIONS
PACIFIC GROVE, CA. 93950-0448

©1986 MIDWEST PUBLICATIONS
PACIFIC GROVE, CA. 93950-0448

FAITH
LOVE
WISH
TRUTH GETGET

©1986 MIDWEST PUBLICATIONS
PACIFIC GROVE, CA. 93950-0448

GARCARAGE
GARCARAGE
GARCARAGE
GARCARAGE

©1986 MIDWEST PUBLICATIONS
PACIFIC GROVE, CA. 93950-0448

1. ~~STOP~~
2. ~~GO~~
3. ~~RUN~~
4. MARCH

©1986 MIDWEST PUBLICATIONS
PACIFIC GROVE, CA. 93950-0448

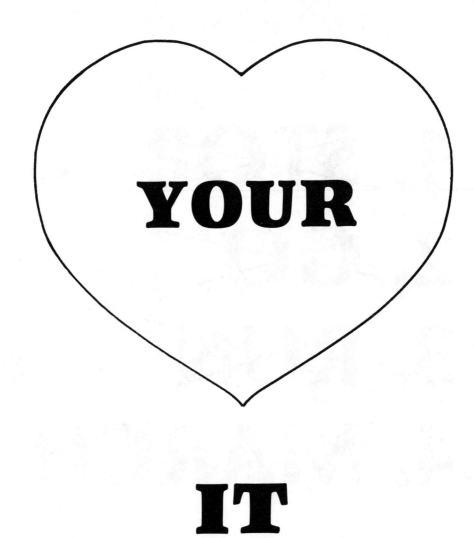

YOUR

IT

©1986 MIDWEST PUBLICATIONS
PACIFIC GROVE, CA. 93950-0448

$$\begin{array}{r} \text{AGE} \\ + \text{ AGE} \\ \hline \end{array}$$

©1986 MIDWEST PUBLICATIONS
PACIFIC GROVE, CA. 93950-0448

HANG
WORD

HANG
WORD

HANG
WORD

HANG
WORD

HANG
WORD

HANG
WORD

©1986 MIDWEST PUBLICATIONS
PACIFIC GROVE, CA. 93950-0448

SCENES STORY

©1986 MIDWEST PUBLICATIONS
PACIFIC GROVE, CA. 93950-0448

SON
SON

©1986 MIDWEST PUBLICATIONS
PACIFIC GROVE, CA. 93950-0448

UMPHUMPHUMPH

©1986 MIDWEST PUBLICATIONS
PACIFIC GROVE, CA. 93950-0448

©1986 MIDWEST PUBLICATIONS
PACIFIC GROVE, CA. 93950-0448

MI NI
SE RI ES

©1986 MIDWEST PUBLICATIONS
PACIFIC GROVE, CA. 93950-0448

GERMAN

ENGLISH

FRENCH

SPANISH

©1986 MIDWEST PUBLICATIONS
PACIFIC GROVE, CA. 93950-0448

THINK-A-GRAM C1

61

©1986 MIDWEST PUBLICATIONS
PACIFIC GROVE, CA. 93950-0448

COMING

COMING

COMING

COMING U COMING

COMING

COMING

COMING

©1986 MIDWEST PUBLICATIONS
PACIFIC GROVE, CA. 93950-0448

B
EANS
BEANSBE
ANSBEANSB
BEANSBEANS

©1986 MIDWEST PUBLICATIONS
PACIFIC GROVE, CA. 93950-0448

PASS
PASS

PASS
PASS

PASS
PASS

GNIKOOL

YEARS

©1986 MIDWEST PUBLICATIONS
PACIFIC GROVE, CA. 93950-0448

NWARD DRAWN ACCOUNT

©1986 MIDWEST PUBLICATIONS
PACIFIC GROVE, CA. 93950-0448

NI ${}^{\text{SHIP}}_{\text{SHIP}}$ GHT

P
U
T
T
I
N
G

I
D
E
A
S
PAPER

©1986 MIDWEST PUBLICATIONS
PACIFIC GROVE, CA. 93950-0448

©1986 MIDWEST PUBLICATIONS
PACIFIC GROVE, CA. 93950-0448

©1986 MIDWEST PUBLICATIONS
PACIFIC GROVE, CA. 93950-0448

RANGER

©1986 MIDWEST PUBLICATIONS
PACIFIC GROVE, CA. 93950-0448

©1986 MIDWEST PUBLICATIONS
PACIFIC GROVE, CA. 93950-0448

D
L
E
H **BURGLAR**

©1986 MIDWEST PUBLICATIONS
PACIFIC GROVE, CA. 93950-0448

GRADE GRADE

GRADE GRADE

GRADE GRADE

GRADE GRADE

GRADE GRADE

GRADE GRADE

GRADUATION

©1986 MIDWEST PUBLICATIONS
PACIFIC GROVE, CA. 93950-0448

OLOGY

©1986 MIDWEST PUBLICATIONS
PACIFIC GROVE, CA. 93950-0448

BLONCEUE
MOON

©1986 MIDWEST PUBLICATIONS
PACIFIC GROVE, CA. 93950-0448

S.H.O.C.K.

THINK-A-GRAM C1

©1986 MIDWEST PUBLICATIONS
PACIFIC GROVE, CA. 93950-0448

ONCE LEAVE

~~TWICE~~

~~THRICE~~

©1986 MIDWEST PUBLICATIONS
PACIFIC GROVE, CA. 93950-0448

BETTING
13579111315...

©1986 MIDWEST PUBLICATIONS
PACIFIC GROVE, CA. 93950-0448

ONESELF   LOOK
LOOK

©1986 MIDWEST PUBLICATIONS
PACIFIC GROVE, CA. 93950-0448

©1986 MIDWEST PUBLICATIONS
PACIFIC GROVE, CA. 93950-0448

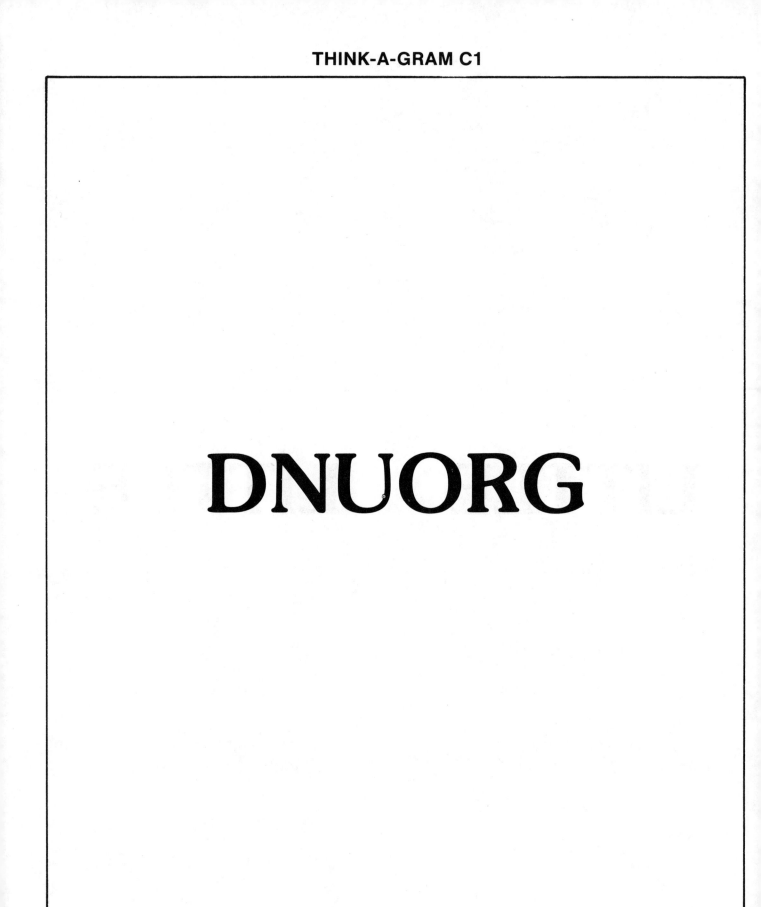

©1986 MIDWEST PUBLICATIONS
PACIFIC GROVE, CA. 93950-0448

©1986 MIDWEST PUBLICATIONS
PACIFIC GROVE, CA. 93950-0448

MY

SPOKEN

©1986 MIDWEST PUBLICATIONS
PACIFIC GROVE, CA. 93950-0448

ONCE

TIME

85

©1986 MIDWEST PUBLICATIONS
PACIFIC GROVE, CA. 93950-0448

©1986 MIDWEST PUBLICATIONS
PACIFIC GROVE, CA. 93950-0448

©1986 MIDWEST PUBLICATIONS
PACIFIC GROVE, CA. 93950-0448

©1986 MIDWEST PUBLICATIONS
PACIFIC GROVE, CA. 93950-0448

©1986 MIDWEST PUBLICATIONS
PACIFIC GROVE, CA. 93950-0448

DAY AT 9:10

©1986 MIDWEST PUBLICATIONS
PACIFIC GROVE, CA. 93950-0448

BAL

BAL

BAL

DANCE

©1986 MIDWEST PUBLICATIONS
PACIFIC GROVE, CA. 93950-0448

UPSET

THINK-A-GRAM C1

©1986 MIDWEST PUBLICATIONS
PACIFIC GROVE, CA. 93950-0448

MOR **DAY** NING

©1986 MIDWEST PUBLICATIONS
PACIFIC GROVE, CA. 93950-0448

PLAFRIENDCE
PLAFRIENDCE

©1986 MIDWEST PUBLICATIONS
PACIFIC GROVE, CA. 93950-0448

©1986 MIDWEST PUBLICATIONS
PACIFIC GROVE, CA. 93950-0448

©1986 MIDWEST PUBLICATIONS
PACIFIC GROVE, CA. 93950-0448

©1986 MIDWEST PUBLICATIONS
PACIFIC GROVE, CA. 93950-0448

BASS
BA
BA

©1986 MIDWEST PUBLICATIONS
PACIFIC GROVE, CA. 93950-0448

R R
NOTHING

©1986 MIDWEST PUBLICATIONS
PACIFIC GROVE, CA. 93950-0448

MEN 2 BOYS

©1986 MIDWEST PUBLICATIONS
PACIFIC GROVE, CA. 93950-0448